Standing with Trees

Poems

Karin Spitfire

The Illuminated Sea Press
2005

Artwork by Rebecca Hazeltine, www. rebeccahaseltine.com
Photo by Peggy McKenna
Book design by Gretchen Warsen

Address orders and correspondence to:
Karin Spitfire
P.O. Box 53
Belfast, ME 04915
kspit@midcoast.com

Printed in Maine

ISBN 0-9761311-5-3

The Illuminated Sea Press
66 Miller St.
Belfast, Maine 04915

This work is dedicated to my family, and with a small light of hope, to the families of veterans of all holocausts, genocides, wars—civil, foreign, domestic, declared, undeclared, global, local, personal… all of us.

Table of Contents

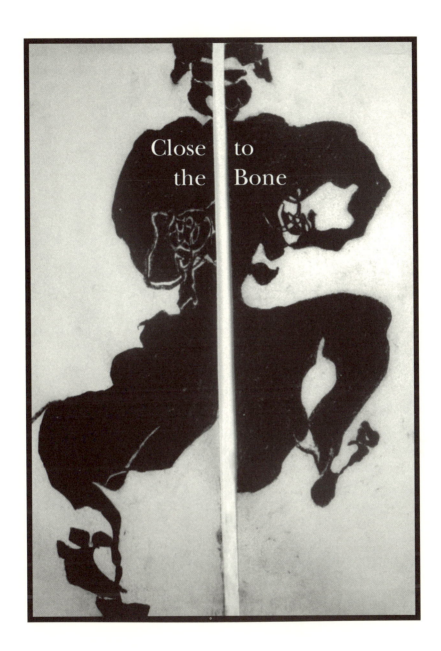

Close to
the Bone

Postcards

When the corn comes in
she always sends postcards
to Japan.

The flavor of sunburst kernels
reminds her of her father's
eyes watching the planes
fly over Pearl Harbor.

She knows how to pick
the ear with the most sweetness,
butter dribbling down her chin.

He can't hold anything without
shaking.

She eats seven ears of his homegrown
organic corn with Blood
Red tomatoes on the side.

They mark their wars with a thousand golden kernels.

Chair

The deerskin
chair sat in the corner
    angled between the fireplace
    and the bay window.

It was the softest thing ever.

My father
    shot the deer
    and upholstered the chair.

    I would curl up in it,
    rubbing my face across the arm
    and gingerly finger the bullet hole
    feeling how much
    I loved and hated

him.

Congress

In my dark-encrusted womb
my father's seed

    does not impregnate me
        but is contained like sand in an oyster.
    it chafes on the
        nuclear membranes of all seven generations.

regardless of the circumstances
the congress has been made.

    it was enough
        that half of me is designed by some lottery of his genes
        molded in the nurture of his terror/ism.

    it was enough
        that he and my mother carried on in
        untouched libraries of first source materials
        that he raped her while i was growing
        in her womb, carrying the eggs
        that would be his granddaughters.

    it was enough
        leaving his mark
        pissing on his territory
        to bind me to him.

he had to move his member
into the last crack

    of course it fit.

Breathing, not

i used to rather die,
or as close to it as you could get
than
        breathe.

i used to rather grey fog bank,
flat land
than
        breathe.

i used to rather graze my cells
in the barest wheeze possible,
than
        breathe
            silver bullet shooting
            through the safety glass shattering
            what was barely held by
            a wobbly shaking frame.

i used to rather pull all my connective tissue
into large tight knots
than
        breathe
            white light terror
            shrieking through fascia
            firing all my nerves.

i used to rather watch from above
than
        breathe
            ripping pain
            burning its way out of
            my intestines.

i used to rather the lead blanket on top of me
than
      breathe
           seething red
           out of control
           i will kill you rage.

i used to rather not

      breathe.

Methods of Murder

I.
I stand before my anatomy class teaching bones and sinew.

The ligamentum nuchae
is a flash of connective tissue,
a finback bone extender off the spinous processes of the cervical vertebrae
to which the most superficial back muscle,
the trapezius is attached;
it exists because there are 152,000
back and neck muscles and by then
we have run out of bony attachment space.

Don't panic: hyperbole, there are only
about 700 muscles in the whole body
most are double, leaving 350.
I don't teach them all, not the
omohyoidius or the pterygoids.
Don't think about muscles now,
we are learning bones.

Innocently, we come to
the bone which makes up a good part of the nose,
the sinuses and supports the third eye,
the ethmoid bone.

I launch into how you can
    kill someone by
    a quick palm up into the nose
    sending the
    ethmoid into the
    sphenoid into the
    brain.

Then there is
the hyoid, the horse shape
bone, which sits in your throat,
    if you hit it likewise with an
    open jab you can
    cut off someone's
    windpipe.

    Or how you can send someone's
Axis (second vertebrae)
    up
    into the base of the skull
    can knock 'em out,
    if not kill them,
since the low brain
controls all the vital functions,
breathing, heart rate, vomiting, consciousness.

I don't list these all in one class,
they just erupt salt and pepper
through the lectures in various classes when we get to
that bone or organ in the outline.

    The kick to the
kidneys,
which are vulnerable, retroperitoneal,
outside of the peritoneum.
    The kick to the
kneecap.
    To the...

These methods of murder come flowing out of my mouth
as natural as nectar from a flower.
I'm in the middle of it long before I recognize my words.

I've never taken self-defense, karate, hand-to-hand combat.
I've never practiced any of these things,

This physical knowing,
    I show the moves,
    they come out of me
in front of the massage/healing students.

One night, late afternoon, dusky fall November,
driving with my father, the long way through the woods, past his rifle range
me and him,
after the woman had been found dead deep in the trees, raped.
Him driving in the dark canopy,
he tells me how to protect myself.

I remember sitting frozen,
"except for the family kidneys, eye sockets, jewels"
written in runes on the concave surfaces of my joints
far out of his reach and my throat.

Thirty years later I'm acting out in front of a class
of mostly women who will walk the line between
massage therapist
or "did you say euphemism for hand job"
adapting the curriculum.

II.
I am on that edge,
I'm in that wild zone of physicality,
where I want to mate,
the mating doesn't begin with any soft tender cheek rub.

It begins with a chase, running through fields, a hunt, a tackle, biting,
scratching, pinning, hollering
not with wanting to get away, escape, but
with the want to connect.
Connect raw wild physical energy,
not banging against each other
banging *with*.

I know the line gets crossed all the time
      that sex/violence line
      embedded in us all after eons
      embedded in my body this lifetime

But I have fury/lust that wants to be met,
to be wrestled with, to be overcome,
to be surrendered to that is
animal, human,
female sexual lust and power.
It has only been stolen, stood on,
appropriated, extorted,
and used against me
It has not ever been let loose, enjoyed or met.

III.
We rented a small freezer locker in Manchester, the next town over. It was
like going to the P.O., with its combination. First go past the H all the way
once to the right, Back counterclockwise past the H to I. Then clockwise to
.... It was the size of a regulation gym locker only deeper and inside a deep
freeze walk-in.
      I went there with my father to drop off the deer he'd shot and butchered
in its labeled white paper packages, or to get out a roast. Venison, I love it.
      It was one more of the places I went alone with my dad. I was the only
one who would cross the line of demarcation. I was glad to be out of the
house Saturday morning and was hoping for some good talks or something.
I went with him to deliver furniture he upholstered, often being left in the
car for unseemly amounts of time.

I'd go with him to the liquor store, which was next to the deli, and sometimes we'd bring home tongue or tripe or some other bizarre thing that I would relish and the rest of the family would do the usual American turn up your nose thing. My dad and I were the eastern europeans, loving caviar, pickled herring, tongue, bananas in sour cream. My mother and brothers, they didn't cross the line.

I was the family envoy to my father. We, my brother, mother and me, were a pack, all against one, braced for the rages, the sneak attacks, the onslaughts. But I crossed the line for years, up until the end actually, when it was over and I told my mother we were leaving or I was going alone.

That was after he took me. I didn't get to use any chops to the hyoid or kicks to the kidneys.

My wild fury/lust was stopped in its tracks; before it even knew there was a bloom.

She Says

She says
every year
for two weeks
she stuffs her nose into lilac blooms.
Impressing her face, herself, with the smell, the delicacy of the petals,
Then she holds the knowledge, the kinesthetic,
the image in herself and waits
for fifty weeks
to do it again.

She does not do this
for only one twelve-month period,
she says,
but year after year.

She takes in, soaks up the lilacs.
Stores them, feeds on the memory of them with delight, anticipation,
patience.

She is renewed,
she says,
with delicious wonder on her daily lilac walks
around the multitudinous lavender hedges of her town.

She is a bee,
she says.
Going from bush to bush.
Why not her nose carrying pollen
no more no less
than the bee.

It is important for her,
she says,
for the lilacs,
that she does this.

What else would she wait for
year after year
for a two-week
woo,
she says?

Rancor

Hopelessness is despair…
>   leaves you prone
>   belly to the ground
>   snake eyed,
>   wailing intermittently.

Faithlessness is suicidal
>   leaves you wandering around
>   whatever environmental desert you're lost in,
>   flat out upright in the vertical plane
>   everything crushing against your face.

My face
>   the trodden bones of the small creature
>   that I grew out of warped,
>   articulations for joining
>   stolen,
>   all the places one might safely allow some hitching,
>   twisted out of shape so that no one,
>   No one…
>   fits in enough ways to stay longer
>   than it takes to find out
>   that behind the façade is a
>   black hole that not even Jesus would enter.

Digestion

when you've bitten off more than you can chew
it takes a long time to digest.

when you've bitten off more than you can chew
or more precisely
when more than you can chew
has been shoved down your throat
it takes a long time to digest.

when more than you can
chew has been shoved down your throat
you have to chew more than you can bite off.

when you have to chew more than you can bite off
when your alimentary tube has been reamed top to bottom and vice versa
the sphincter muscles, the epithelial linings and all the nerve endings
are confused every time you eat.
every time you eat
the gagging, barfing and scared shitless sensors are activated
every time it is time to eat,
the gauntlet has to be fooled.

when what has been shoved down your throat
is more than you can stomach
it takes a long time
for the weight of food to calm the nerves
for the blood to infuse tube linings
for the muscles to motor smoothly
to take in what is needed, to know what is not
to relax the sphincters.

it takes a long time
for gut reactions to be restored
for all the natural acts to regain instinct.
it takes a long time to recognize food
for eating to become eating.

the daily to be regular and
for digesting the regular, daily

then
having spit out as much as you can,
digesting what was shoved down your throat daily
takes a long time
    a lot of chewing, masticating, gnawing, foaming at the mouth
    a lot of swallowing what is hard to swallow
    a lot of churning, churning what is hard to stomach
    a lot of sorting, not that, nor that, no not that, yes that.
    that little crumb, and that bit will nourish
    a lot of irritable bowel
    a lot of letting go.

it takes a long time for the pile of garbage
that has been shoved down your throat
to become the load of shit it always was.

The day my father dies

There will be pie,
green tomato pie, blueberry, peach, raspberry, apple, mince, strawberry,
apricot -mango, kiwi lime pie, and fig pie.
　　There will be a piece for everyone.

The day my father dies
　　We will sing and dance in the streets.

　　The wounded, oversized, uncontainable,
　　lumbering, vicious mad man is dead.
　　The ones whose hearts ache too much to soften,
　　The mush balls, carrying the grief of dead men
　　unable to cry for themselves, each other, their children,
　　unable to cry for a millennium of
　　stiff upper lip manhood
　　of learning not to cry at three.

The day my father dies
　　The ties, the anchors, the knots, the nooses, the chains, the hooks
　　will go to the blacksmith shop and be heated, pounded into
　　scrap metal.

The day my father dies,
　　for a week we will pack up
　　the catalogued immercies, the ugliness,
　　the truth of his legacy and his before him
　　the scrapbook of bloodstains
　　fist marks, bruises, visible and invisible
　　the CD with the reverb of his voice cut on our cell's membranes
　　the home video of the hypervigilence, the special effects of being fast
　　enough
　　to escape the belt, running around and around
　　in his house, placing everything where he demanded
　　avoiding the crushing plaster of his body.
　　We will pack up all of the need in his eyes,
　　the yearning to express his love and

the soft untouchable place
my preciousness provoked to raging.

We will burn it all with him and
the ashes we will bury.

> Nature will rejoice to receive such compost,
> She will
> metabolize all the WWII heroes and losers,
> all the cold war queens.
> We will be left with only their children, vietnam and ours, iraq.

Freedom will ring.
> We will know the past is the past and the cleanup is as good as it gets.

After that only one in every 23 poems will make reference to him.
The scars will only pulsate yearly on the day he died
and we will all eat pie.

Oh my daddy, he loved pie.

Healing from trauma is Poetry

healing from trauma is working
in the soul's emergency room,
leaks everywhere from antipersonnel bombs
bloody, messy,
where is the wound, can we stanch this one
here is another,
how to make it out of ICU to rehab?

but souls don't heal in ICU or lockdowns,
the kind hands are covered with latex
the walls are too white,
the medicine afraid of spirit
unable to differentiate symptom
from cause.

healing from trauma
is putting together
one of those new fangled three-dimensional
jigsaw puzzles,
with the added problem of time
wavering back and forth
and a guarantee of missing pieces.

healing from trauma is a
poem.

healing from trauma
is poetry
you sorta kinda understand,
maybe,
what?

healing from trauma
is a saga.
oh, that it was a
haiku.

healing from trauma is
the libretto of an italian opera
    with balkan women singers as the backup
    african drummers and dancers the chorus line
    lakota warriors and belly dancers with virtuoso solos
    cameos of irish step dances, russian cossacks,
    the whole thing surrounded by tibetan monks and yoginis at a distance
    with gale force winds of emotion playing the orchestra.

you sing all the major roles,
    the dead, the shaman, lost soul, villain, hag, whore, prima donna,
    scapegoat, confidant, innocent bystander and the hero.
you rehearse each separately, every other week for years
we can only tolerate the full complement occasionally
you are always slightly off-key, out of balance
    erupting, gagging, shivering, stammering.

this opera is simulcast
done while having a virtual life in the present
without the music,
without the supporting cast,
you will not get through.

healing from trauma is an italian opera turned epic
healing from trauma is aria-ating it as many times as necessary.
it is a long run.

then leaving,
walking out of the theater.

    without any acknowledgment of heroism...
    no golden fleece,
    not even one Myth of killing your father,
    avenging your honor, winning the kingdom.

healing from trauma is its own award

healing from trauma
is poetry
you sorta kinda understand,
maybe,
what?

Equilibrium

I am a mule train.

One mule loaded, carrying the burden, packages, supplies, winding down the canyon wall.

Winding, careful one step, one hoof, please, one after another, each hoof testing the ground, how close, how firm the edge, plodding down, using the necessities and unloading the burden bit by bit.

Go, carefully. Do not fall off the edge. Reaching into ledges for a meal, for a rest.

Watching the light change, get less with the descent. Fragile moments of daylight brilliance bouncing off the walls. In the beginning it shone on me, now there is only high up illuminated patches.

Twisting and turning, heading down the path, the narrow prescribed random water wash, wind etched canyon track. Down, shedding burdens. Rocks loosen under foot and fall the long way, crashing below.

The mule train years are at an end. I have gone down the canyon with my burden. I am at the bottom. My bottom. The wash. Canyon walls close in on every side. Light, stars, high above.

I thought I was a mountain goat. Going up the crags and crannies edge, finding foothold, finger grip, belly to ledge. A mountain goat, ascending and looking up, stretching for the next crevasse, legs pushing up over around the boulder strewn path. A goat not looking back past all that I left behind or at the heights I have reached.

Looking up, going up, moving out, past, beyond where I came from, traveling, searching, reaching, one step at a time up the hill, up the mountain slope, no apparent path, no apparent top, just the edge, just the lead, just digging in one heel, one toehold, hand over hand arm hoisting pulls, going up trying to get a view of what was possible, trying to reach something else that I knew was possible. Something that had to have a lot of space, had to see the light.

A mountain goat, afraid of heights, with no brook for the yawning abyss behind me, looking ahead, listening for the sounds of freedom, going, going. If you could keep pace with me, I'd tell you what I see as I go by.

A mountain goat at the top, there are vistas for the eyes, and only the peak for foothold.

But no, I am mule, gone down, shifting the burdens, necessities, using them up, grinding on them like the wind and water on sandstone. I am at the bottom now, (and one hesitates to say that, Malvina Reynolds "so you think you've hit bottom" refrain bursting into my head).

I am at the bottom. Let me tell you this is not a bad place. All the burdens are gone, they have either been tossed off, or masticated into use…

it is not true completely that all the burdens are gone, there is the grit in the teeth, the sand in the hair, eyelashes, weathered skin, aching joints. And yes, there is sneaking residue of guilt at making it in the corners of microvillus, and the smelly old habit of trying to stop the wall from being wall…

but it is the end of the path, there is nowhere to go this way.

> Up or down,
> on the edge,
> close to the wall,
> either way.
> The bottom,
> surrender all the details, wait.
> The top,
> space, free.
>
> The bottom
> only a different path
> or the wall.
> The top,
> only death,
> catching its whiff in your memory,
> or descent.

Meanwhile, at the range of sea level, every time I awake I find an infinite variation of flowers, greens, and wild life. All these years, I have lived here at sea level, at the ocean's wide horizontal to provide the long pole for my soul's

>   Ascent
>   decent,
>   return.

There is balance,   in every direction.   You can trust it.

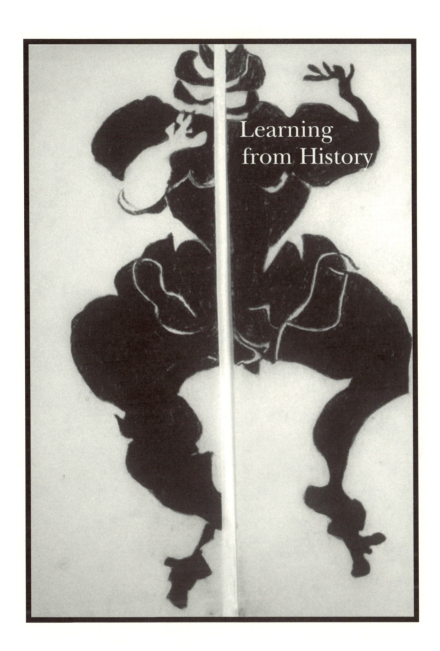

Learning
from History

Hope

flashes like a man in a trench coat
penis dangling
now you see it, now you don't
the after image, neon, repetitive

a shadow passes over your
core, ephemeral but with
all the hooks of a twelve-dollar lure

it does not take you down;
when it happens you are already
out for the count.
it is the billboard over hollywood announcing
"I don't want to live like this"

    in the valley of the shadow of death, rather die

it catches on everything,
eviscerates at any moment
grabs you by the short hairs of your soul
you have done your best to wear smooth all the edges where it might catch
but
it just has to pass across the sun like a cloud

darting across your essence in the morning
between wake and sleep
when you are defenseless and corrupt.

the faintest, fleeting glimpse
snares every cell
you are riveted
    despondency lies behind your being
    but even that is too much action
if you struggle it will crush you
you know you must wait,
for it has had you on your knees before
you do not eat, you do not move for fear it will find you.

you get up with dread
you are pinned like a butterfly
you have to move from the board all day.

CAN I GET YOU ANOTHER COCKTALE ?

I pretend my favorite Cocktail is Molotov
but frankly my resistance hasn't taken up arms
I've taken up hems, padded bras, left my hair unspiked,
I've passed.

I don't drink the stuff
I just serve it.

I have proof/100 proof
    I can give it to you straight up
            on the rocks
            blended/unblended
            with a twist
    any way I think you might hear it.

I can even give it to you watered down,
which some would say was a sign of my healing.

But the fact of the matter is I don't want to give it to you at all.
And I certainly don't want you to give it to me,
    I've had it: sideways
            backwards
            up side the head
            on a silver platter once
            by the sea
            behind closed doors
            but mostly in public with shame.

I want it to stop
    We have proof,
    Any way you take it: Black, with cream and sugar, decaffeinated
            anthropological
            medical
            historical

legal
ontological
By God
By Nature
By logic
We have said it: nice, yelling, in the streets, in seminars,
in the bedroom, at court, in meetings.
till we are
Blue in the face
seeing Red
turned green
vomiting
scared to death,
gone crazy,
made amends.

I have gone around the world,
jumped through hoops of fire,
Retreated,
licked my wounds.
I have changed every Cell in my body.

AND YOU'RE STILL HAVING BABIES FOR BREAKFAST.

The last cocktail I serve I would like to put down with
a sound
that ignites the hair
on your body
into a fast quick conflagration which just reaches your skin
and lets you sit in the stench, the pain, and
Know the meaning of Terror.

I should want to kill you
but your favorite fix will do it for you.

My job is to not serve myself up as proof.

Waiting

waiting for the brush of the cheek against cheek,
    the soft gentle nuzzled lips finding lips.
waiting for the breath intake, the small panting,
    the first delicate flicker of the tongue.
waiting for the moment when you separate,
    come up for air, and
this time dive ever so slightly,
deeper
into the realms of taking in, giving over, mixing it up.

waiting for the first time
your tongue finds
    the corner of the lips,
    the other's tongue,
waiting for the moment that it can't be stood any longer
    and the hand that has been brushing the nape of your neck wraps into
    your hair and pulls you into a big full-lipped,
    full tongue wet dive.

waiting,
the kind of waiting that could take days, or hours, or
that timeless time of waiting for the hand, the tongue to follow
    the ripples sent out by the first kiss
    crashing in and overlapping on each other till the
    dive reaches the milky way

waiting for the cells and molecules to reorganize into some
semblance of form that you knew to be you,
knew to be the other kisser,
but has retuned to time and space inextricably altered.

that's worth waiting for.

Play

When I weed I play Vietnam,
I defoliate.
I push the hoe, I chop the
heads off those weeds, I am
a guillotine.
I jab, stab, dig at their roots.
Get the roots
failing that, off with their heads.

When I weed I play fascism
leave only the single row of baby carrots,
beets, lettuce.
Take away the chickweed, lambsquarters, galensoga, sour grass, dandelions,
rag weed,
sorrel, nutritious edibles.
Leave only the
basil.

I go after those weeds, with the hand hoe, the push hoe, the hula hoe.
I turn my anger,
my desire to be a terrorist,
to gun down the boards of the Fortune 500
on the weeds.

It does not matter. I could pull them out with loving kindness.
It does not matter if I am weeping or laughing,
they just come up again
or are replaced by others just the same.

I Can't Tell You This

i can't tell you how my spirits rise,
that it is december
and instead of being forty degrees
raining, damp, with forsythia blooming

it is snowing.
it was a squall, fleeing the sky where the sun was still shinning.
it was nothing,
now the sky blue is gone, the sun is gone, above is grey and big flakes are
falling
it is december, i am home
my house is a mess
i can stop tracking, ordering the details of multilevel needs.
i can stay in the dream, it is winter, it will be dark, i have candles,
there is a fire burning, sagittarius reigns,
no one is calling me out of the dream

I cannot tell you

outside my dream
float
near-dead bodies, I am swimming among lost souls,
bumping up against each other,
I know how to swim, I know the water is too cold,
I have gotten back in, voluntarily.
how can I tell you, what the waters are like, I don't know the raw details.
I know the truth.

I am fishing for souls, they float hover around the bodies,
nets, hooks, draggers, don't have any yield.

I can't tell You or Him
How some jungle,
    wading through the bodies of the fallen,
    enemies and buddies alike...
    no one caring if You lived
    through the melée,
    only that when it was over
    Your side had gained what?

I can't tell
How some jungle,
    That has no resemblance to a five room track house,
    charcoal grey with turquoise shutters,
    kitchen table with
    barely a seven-year-old's width
    behind the father's chair and the wall.

are the same.
are not the same.

You trust your senses,
I say that's all there is

You
come home,
all of us
have sent
You,
we enjoy our cars, and the endless list of days filled with
not seeing how simple it would be....

the fragile wrap of flesh
we are.
to be killed or kill,

I don't know what ocean Your soul is in

but My kind
    no one sent us anywhere,
    there was no foreign territory,
    there was no "social gain."
    We feed the small hungry causes
    that lived in the place
    called home.

    We were torn apart by
    our "own" flesh and blood,
    We did not carry guns,
    We did not "stand" a chance,
    They did not need to carry guns,
    just bodies, perogative
    and lust filled with some kind of
I cannot tell you
    that did not have to invade, conquer,
    just took,
    like swatting a fly, grabbing a beer out of the fridge, hollering
    to the one in the kitchen for more.

Your life depended on killing.
    My kind
    depended on the big hand
    wrapped around us like a noose, if we struggled, expanded,
    breathed it would pull tighter.

Both called crazy,
You antisocial,
    Us, they have made an industry out of Our pain.
    one of the things
You protected,
    their right to not see the truth.

I have yet to see one of Us, Your or My kind
    whose "insanity"
    whose behavior is not
    illuminated by the actual detail
    of the act and circumstances of the...

I can't tell you.

You stay alive by not "going there"
    You saw it all,
    once.
    every detail etched, every sense.
My senses worked until there was no hope but escape....
    We did not see it,
    it got whited out by terror,
    blotted out by labyrinths of retreat.
Maybe, You could move, had to with your gun,
Maybe, We were great Houdinis,
    our souls
    finding a way out of our bodies
    no matter the trap. the knots.
    I had to lie still, act dead, find the door out the back of my navel.
    the cave entrance,

I cannot tell you

how the layers of days upon days,
I know exactly
the place where the stones with garnets were in the stone wall, the order of
how His tools were hung in the garage, the placement of the petrified wood
ashtray on the coffee table, how His top drawer looked, a pile of folded
ironed white cotton handkerchiefs, a shoe horn, nail clippers, wallet,
arranged. our baby pictures smiling at Him as he opened it. the line between
His side of the closet and Hers. the wood gun case under the bed.
the wallpaper in My bedroom grey background abstract horseshoe designs in
aqua and pink with gold dots randomly scattered. the order of the canned

goods under the staircase, next to the box that had the green quilted heavy
upholstery blanket, the exact place in the basement. in front of the stored
screens, next to the water heater, in behind His worktable. in there.
how many days of it
listening to the speed of the garage door opening, how much slam was there
on the way down, the cadence of His steps up the stairs, how close was din-
ner to being ready.
the days He was recovering from a hernia, on the sunporch, the only way
into the house.
the days He was sleeping when we got home because He worked swing shift.
the days of not having a piece of paper on the floor, of not finishing the
peanut butter, of listening at one a.m. for His set of steps. would He give me
warm milk and honey for my insomnia, sit with me. would he ignore me.
would He...
the days i would cross over the enemy lines and go with Him on His errands,
to deliver furniture, to the deli to buy tongue, head cheese, to the liquor
store, to the freezer locker to get venison.
the days
how many days on duty,
no furlough, no RR, no leave,
the years zero to 16, the years of watching the prevailing wind,
preparing for the storms, will it be a hurricane, a blizzard, a flash flood.

my ears, my eyes are not worn out.

I cannot tell you.

How does an infant, or you name the age,
stand in a house like any other house,
a yard, not a jungle, not a foreign territory,
not an environment where you can see a battle was fought.
Recognize,
Her body as the battlefield, Her soul as the territory,
the provider, the one
She is hormonally designated to love, the enemy
how does She come home.

I don't know how You come home either,

He supposedly came home, from a different war.

> i come home, i walk in the door, the house is a mess,
> here i only have to feed my own soul…
> done swimming for the week, i know where the ladder out of the pool is.
> it is snowing over the ocean...
> i have my own
> four walls, coffee table, basement.

how many days
I can't tell you.

I can't tell you
the cost.

> i can't tell you how in my own four walls, protected, safe,
> i suffer, how i miss my father,
> how i am jealous that no one is patting my head and hugging me when i
> am scared,
> how i am grateful for the walls, grandma's chair, the money to buy the
> candles, the wood, the view.

> i can't tell you how happy i am that the snow has thickened
> i can't see town anymore across the bay. that i can get that winter
> hibernation feeling, dream, knit, bake a pie, write
> i can't tell you how poignant and impossible life is.

Amygdala/Learning from History
(for Bessel van der Kolk)

All it takes is a sonic boom
them practicing the art of war
called defense
that slight of hand offense

    my father guarded
    your peaceful sleep
    his nightmares re-occurred
    no camouflage needed

    all it took was a mosquito invasion
    in our screenless house
    for the planes
    to reappear in his eyes

    my father was a terrorist, a hit man
    he was not the tyrant,
    he was not the armchair sportsman
    cheering on the boys.

    all it took was a break in the sound barrier
    for him to jump my bones
    his rifle butt in my gut
    his left thumb in my throat

All it takes is a sonic boom
for me to jump and run.
I was taught to love
freedom more than safety.

How to Practice Not Becoming Voiceless/Speechless
When Shock Occurs
And/Or One Way To Practice Releasing Shock

Jump Naked
    into the Ocean
        in Maine
Come Up
    Squealing
      Screaming.

You can begin on the hottest days
    early to mid-August.
      when the air will help you.
In a shallow cove
    just after low tide, mid-afternoon
      when the sun has baked the rocks in her zenith
      and the water has sucked up the heat.

You can go on practicing as the water reaches its warmest
    in the end of August, but the air has cooled
      on through September
        Now hardier and *hardly* needing to yelp
          but doing so for the pure pleasure of it.

You can practice this, beginning earlier, July, next year
    til eventually you know the earlier the plunge
      the sooner the cobwebs of winter will leave your tissues
      and the more swimming will be had.
You can practice
    til you finally join Mary York at Curtis Cove every May 31.

Practice
    til you love it
      and it just is,
        except when you're trapped in one of those conversations with
        awestruck tourists and you can't help yourself.

When you have all that under your belt

Jump Naked
    into
        Lake Superior.

By practicing thusly,
    you will have lost all idiotic injunctions for stiff upper lips and not crying or
        howling when you fall, crash head to cement off your bike in Amsterdam,
        or the man at the table pinches your cheek.
            You will come up screaming.
            The shock will not freeze you.

want

to be in a grownup sexual relationship—
where sex is all things.

where sex is regular,
sometimes tender, deep, soul-matching surrender,
sometimes a quick hot fuck,
sometimes cozy comfort,
an antidote to despondency,
sometimes too much wicked fun, animal, mammal, tease,
sometimes anything that doesn't land you in the hospital,
the longest sniff of every cell, the smoothest silkiest sensuous meltdown,
sometimes a flashback
sometimes an outpouring of grief.

where sex is everything
silk stockings, bustier and garters,
holey long johns,
sometimes you doing nothing except purring,
me being pinned.
sometimes simply cunt wrapped around penis tongue deep in mouth now.

where sex is everything

but always just you and me
not any of the ex-lovers, we can toast to them in our acts but that's it.
no third parties allowed, no other women, no other men, not your mother,
my father,
no relatives watching through portholes, no commentary from the peanut
gallery,
no voyeurs
just me and you
listening/reading each other like one good book after another
sometimes this kind of a novel, heroine, siren
sometimes that kind of a warrior, soft exposed neck surrender
where sex is everything
but anybody else's business.

You can get There from Here

I.
your mind's eye
imagines something else,
it has no name other than
better, not this.

you know it's possible.
you can taste it.
it has no evidence,
still there's a vague memory
or prescience.

your body's eye feels for it,
something different.

it is a physical search
having only will,
the will to escape, to not succumb,
wrought by wolves biting at your heels.

you go.

II.
you learn to ski,
you understand, in kind,
how to look.

approximating, guessing, watching others,
trial and error,
when you've found it once,
felt it,
it's a new world.
you can go for the feeling,
call to muscle, bone and nerve
to retrace the new groove,
feel that nascent place.

from here getting to there
regardless of the tools you've found or mastered.

you are always breaking trail.
you have to go around great bodies of water,
wade through logjams, negotiate rapids.
you just have to paddle,
snowshoe, and bushwack.

III.
until you get to the salt marsh
of your own intertidal pools and rest
letting the water
pour in fresh, the
sea rise and ebb
diluting, carrying away the toxins
tide by tide,
balancing the brackish fresh mix,
the bittersweet pH, letting the
macrophages work
slowly
diminishing the number of cells
that think you yourself are
the enemy.

here the sea breeze massages the grasses,
fills the red oxygen carriers with breath
and lifts away your exhale.

here the mud is teeming
with generativity,
reminding each cell of its
daughters born
here
in this sieve between earth and sea.

born here now,
not then, not back there.

many good storms
help the remix,
the marsh matter holds firm
even as it is rearranged.

IV.
until this continual refreshing chemical soup
has seeped into
and cleared bone, softened muscle,
reoriented each organ away from
hurricane watch to temperate moontide
fill and empty,

til the mind's body
recognizes joy.

til body's mind can turn away from the
sticky, protruding, deafening
claw of violence and its offspring.

turn away, or
hold ground,
not denying the screeching
but refusing to take the bait,
preferring the birthright
joy
to any brass ring.

Backfires

I.
I was falling asleep praying,
    Praying to that sort of Bigness, that engulfing Bigness
    I saw when my mother died,
for a miracle in the Middle East.

As I was praying to
a transcendent out there-over us kind of Bigness,
it collapsed.
Came kaleidoscoping down like my father's mess kit cup, fitting
all into itself.

Off to one side, zooming in
came this other spiritual belief that I hold,
We are all one.

If we are all one,
then I had to pray to the rest of the humans
on the planet
and it was up to us.

I collapsed into sobbing.
It is up to us.

I heard Anne ring the Bell and say that Buddhist line
May all sentient Beings awake.
I knew what it meant for the first time,
what a prayer it is,
What a Prayer It Is
MAY ALL SENTIENT BEINGS AWAKE

The next day,
my aversion to humans I had to lose.
It is up to us.

What is most important when I know myself as co-creating the universe?

The next day,
it all backfires when
I wake up with an aversion to myself.

II.
Back Fires.
The back fires behind the lines,
where the women who follow
the troops
cook, wash, boil sheets for bandages, blankets for lice, onions for broth.
the back fires, behind the lines.

The lines can't be drawn anymore.
We carved out Israel, the Arabs all around refuse the Palestinians, the
Palestinians stay, the Arabs refuse to recognize Israel, Israel refuses to recog-
nize Palestine.
Blood is cast, spilled over and over.
The beat goes on.
The lines cannot be drawn,
women and children, girls and boys
and men and old men, everywhere.

No one is not a soldier.
No one is not in the lines.
No one is not a victim.
No one is not a victim.
It backfires, every bomb, every attack,
backfires
kills more of our own.
All of us.

III.
I am getting countless redundant requests for money from the Sierra Club,
the Wildlife Federation, the Natural Resource Council, the Heifer Project,
Save the Children, End World Hunger, Keep Abortions Safe, NOW, United
Farm Workers, Civil Liberties Union, the democratic party.

They are all acting as if everything should just go on the same.
As if THEIR strategy was NEEDED NOW more than ever,
that they shouldn't take a look at themselves after September 11.

No one is saying on 911 the bell rang, Wake up.
They are Saying how the world has changed and doing more of the same.
Send US money to save the arctic,
the rain forest, the tiger, the panda, the whale, the rights, the child.
Give US money to reform elections.

From, if we can call it that — the other side —
I am getting countless offers for credit cards, 0% for 6 months,
4.9% for the life of the loan, citibank, firstbank, mbna, first card, chase, first
national bank.
They are all giving me a debt offer.
Do my part of the strings and mirror dance,
to shore up the economy
in the NAME of freedom and democracy,
for the richest of the rich
consolidated abuse of power
in the most life-on-the-planet-risking manner.
AND WHAT EXACTLY HAS CHANGED?

There are no lines.
There are no behind the lines,
plenty of behind the scenes.

Power mongering,
greed frenzy feeding.
The sharks are all swimming
called out by the Blood.

IV.
There are no lines. It is all Just Backfiring
We've all got the same blood lines
Four little proteins, a tetragrammaton, proliferating every living thing on
the Planet
human blood just backfiring on ourselves and every other living...

The only way to fall out
is into
something different,

kissing
the hard truth
It is up to us.

Hold Fire

Hold Fire.
you there,
yes,

You have to
hold fire.
hold your fire.
hold your own fire.

Do contain it.
be a vessel.
hold fire.

Do not look to the generals, the man above.
do not look for the other side's white flag.

Hold fire.

Yes, you.
You have the job.
The job of managing your fire, your own fire
    of keeping it going enough so you have spirit, action,
    of not letting it get damped down so as to go out
    or so hot you shoot out raging flames that burn into

    flesh,
    out of control fires

    you can fan flagging souls,
    you can ignite, inspire, jump start, spark
    conversation, creativity, woodstoves, campfires,
    melodies, tall tales, remembarances.

Holding Fire is a lesson,
    how many times do you have to get burned,
    how many times do you have to jump through the flames,

walk over hot coals
to get the vessel annealed, tempered enough to Hold Fire.

You know when to hold fire.
Those moments when you flare and it lands on dry hay, parched forest,
frazzled bedfellows

Oil Fields.

Energy conservation starts at home.

In the army they get you all juiced up.
Get you all going at the gooks and ginks, cunts and pussies.
They punish you, humiliate, shame, beat you.
Pour rage into you to contain, temporarily.
They call it basic training.
Their way of hardening, toughening you up,
so you can hold fire
theirs and yours.
Until
They
decide the right moment
to yell FIRE.
                        We all know you do not
                        yell Fire in a movie theater…
                        the planet is a movie theater.

Don't fire.
See the whites of their eyes,
the mirror in the pupils.
hold fire.

Hold your Fire,
your life spark.
It is a big job, big enough for anybody.
Why would you give it to someone else to hold?

Why would you set it loose on someone else's demand?

Oh yeah, they put the gun to your head.
Is he holding his fire?
Who's holding whose?
    enough oil
    enough grease, fat
    one spark.

fire, hold your Fire
be a light
not a shot.

Aikido
(for Len Cohen)

There is good and evil.
There is no sense in collapsing this into oneness.

The trick of evil
is to get you to think
that it balances good,
that it is the equal and opposite force of good.

Evil is a speck in the enormity of good.

The trick of evil
is to get you to focus on it,
to give it energy by hating it, warding it off, fearing it.
In this way of pulling you to it, evil grows and feeds itself.

The way to deal with evil is to Love.

Love what you love. Love yourself.
Love yourself to death.
All the way to death if it comes to that.
It will one way or another.

Healing

It's like knitting

> you don't want to drop any
> stitches, but
> of course you do
> how long does it take to notice?
> a couple of rows,
> when you're experienced

> but some stitches were dropped long ago
> when you didn't know any better
> when that color yarn wasn't
> when you didn't know it was missing

> years later, after randomly following
> directions you didn't understand
> being led by your nose
> through brambles, raspberry patches,
> wide-open spaces without
> markings

> > someone
> > from
> > somewhere
> > else
> > brings
> > fresh figs and cream
> > to the table

> the crochet hook finds the
> lost stitch
> slowly and steadily
> pulls up through space
> the missing.
> it is tough,

all the other threads
tightening

miraculously it reaches the present
after a little wear the
tension of the whole
evens out

        a stitch
        is just the right twist in
        a long line of yarn
        filling a gap.

Meditation Lesson

I sit balancing
on the fence
filigree metal,
Italian ornate
lacking symmetry.

I have wrestled
myself here
from a life
on the edge
of the void.

It is an improvement.

On the fence
the void is on both sides
but the locus of perception
has moved to center.

Body Memory

We have all gone over and over again to the grove trees, to the fire, to the rhythm, to the foot stomping-arm waving, voice-raising circles for communion. We have all gone over and over again to the clearing of the air, to the moving mass of us in authentic unison freeing the "evil spirits." Freeing the possessed, condensed, coagulated, depressed. Freeing from ruminating and clogging the "to be opened and emptied spaces" of our body-mind. We have done it over and over again, in the name of gods and goddesses, spirits, fairies, cosmologies, to realign, clear out, open up, clarify.

We have over and over again created and passed down messy unattainable structures, loose, formal, strict, precise, with small coats of transparencies to hold the numinous, to balance the multi-diversity of oneness.

We have created and practiced forms, egg dying, sand painting, lei making, yoga, tai chi, hora to call home to ourselves the light shimmering in the grain of rice, the fresh life bursting under our tongues as we crush new greens between our teeth. We have given thanks over and over again for the nourishment of the bright berries eaten by the wild deer, the precious egg.

We have fasted, made flower offerings, killed the lamb. We have rolled naked in the fields drunk with springs bursting to mix the gene pool.

Over and over again we have done this to right-size ourselves in the face of our powerlessness and the glorious nature of our existence.

We have reminded ourselves, daily, weekly, at the equinoxes, solstices, at the births and deaths, of our best examples.

We have done it in the hallowed diversity of the lands we inhabit and in the sounds rising up into language. We have all done it.

And we have done it longer than Allah's revelation to Mohammed, the resurrection of Christ, or the enlightenment of Buddha.

We have done it longer than the secularization of any act of production, before the day of rest and devotion fell away from feeding the baby, making the tortillas, weaving the baskets, arranging flower hats to wear up the mountain and place at the foot of the goddess.

We have done it with the seamlessness of dawn breaking on the horizon with a great shout at the rising orb's appearance. We moved in and out of the tides of need, expression, worship, art, utility, with the relentlessness and uniqueness of the waves on long sand beaches or granite pounded edges.

And we are still called every day, every day past the edge of materialism, past the edge of language, to joyfully acknowledge the spiritual essence of our physicality and to act accordingly.

Standing with Trees

Prayer: How to Think about the Body

I.   A vibration
nesting in an echo chamber
repeating, reverberating your soul's work.

A tympanic orchestra,
a string quartet, a tube of tubas, clarinets, horns

A vibration that hears sky, land, trees, cars,
reconstitutes and transforms
every movement.

II.   A billion twinkling firelights,
spark flames

not doused, but nurtured by
water

within soft filigree
earth sacs

the whole thing leavened by
tiny air balloons

and spiced with
minerals.

III.   A membrane that balances pressures
barometric, air, gravity, water, financial, family
from one side,
or vice versa

a membrain that reads lips, hears totems, touches infinity, and
forges alliances with rock, heat, aol.com, and thoughts.

IV.   Membranes
encircling DNA serpents
making every cell drum
spiraling through liquid seas

Membrains
banking the waters that flow in their deltas
molding earth muscle flesh
holding chemical lightning nerves,
and icing the crystallized snow bones.

V.   A quaking bag of liquid fire, oxygenated earth, walking around,
skipping through three-dimensional space
making time.

Faith

I.
she said
don't worry
you only see white light.

I wondered
how she knew
both things.
that anytime I was asked to visualize
I only saw white light, and
that I worried about this.

oh yes, when someone tells me their story or is in the middle of a flashback,
I see a room, the wallpaper, shape, color of tablecloth,
I do not know if these are "accurate" but I do know they are not mine.

but, when they say visualize yourself walking down a staircase,
sitting in your favorite place, or at the beach,
I see only white light. no pictures. no colors.

oh yes, sometimes when someone stands before me,
I can see their bones in a kind of x-ray light.
or in a certain unexpected knowing make the sound that vibrates the pain
away,
or find the release by touch of the unseen tension.

but, when they say visualize, I see only white light,
brilliant full blast,
or smooth abalone shell glistening with a hint of color, or sparkling white
Starburst surrounded by black.

II.
when my mother died,
I saw the white light firmament. Like the movies.
ONLY BIGGER,
vast, the firmament of white light and love.

Love bigger than all of the holocausts known to me,
in their overwhelming unbelievability, pain, anguish,
but specks in this light.
there are no words for this,
I'm sorry I can't translate,
I can hardly reckon the holotropic experience
except for the fact of it,
and remember a faint taste of the feeling, an imprint,
the glad thing it was.

III.
the other night
I was in pain
physical
the fascia gone fascist, taut, tense, nonpliable
stiff, achy, no fluids moving.

I dreamed my mother
came to minister to me
she gently stroked my fingers
slightly pushed into them and said
breathe rainbows through your cell membranes.

when I woke, "of course!" I said,
fluids passing through the translucent
membranes of the cells, of the connective tissue
would make rainbows as they pass.
refracted, reflected through the shapes of the molecules.

so when you look at the sun diamond sparkling off the
waves on the water, and see the hints of rainbow, so it is as
the tides ebb and flow through our cells.

Writing

Weeding by hand,
even if you take up the roots with a big swath of your hand hoe,
you still have to pick each weed out, one at a time
or it will re-root and grow again.

The feathery carrot tops, each one, the chosen, stay.

They were there all along, hidden,
the straight row of words, one right after the other.
All the divergent green distractions cleared away
so you can see the one line,

the small, crystallized essence of this one thought.

May 3

red tips of bud are
on the winter skeleton trees
when I leave home.

waking in a spot
a minute warmer, a degree south
there in the sky is
green,
baby leaf chartreuse
tenderest new.

the softest tiny see-through
life green
fluttering feathery in the air.

my pulse leaps,
startled to see green
so thoroughly accommodated to
winter sentinel, lovely, bare naked trees.

now there is the frilly dress,
the baptismal lace
a sound too fresh to miss.

gasps escape me
my lungs fill,
and moan the last moan,
I can breathe again, open
the air is to be renewed.

the alveoli,
the tiny pink air sacs of lung
rejoice at the return of
their twin sister.

Knitters

Hearsay has it that
the guy who invented computers
did so from watching his wife knit.
that hypnotic both-hands work
that frees the mind.

A binary system, knit, purl
one string, one stitch after another,
a linear form, two options
an infinite variety of pattern.

Every pattern has a map,
some have charts
and like all good navigating systems
the charts have abbreviations, definitions, scale,
and tension.

The one I'm working now has
a chart for rows 1 to 4
pattern panels for 1-8
which then repeat while
shaping the back, pockets, sleeves,
front, collar.

Every time I pick it up, I have to reorient
the work to map to chart to definitions,
check for the right row in the correct panel
of the proper pattern.

Knitters move
left to right, english
right to left, hebrew
bottom to top, not chinese.

Having figured out how to make a dualistic,
two-dimensional system

into beautiful designs of
three-dimensional utilitarian objects,
knitters engage both sides of the brain
building the corpus callosum
keeping the hands busy,
while the mind flies, ruminates, and dreams.

When I knit my mind goes to a virtual reality
of my own making. When I'm done
I have something warm to wear and you
can read the code when I walk down the street.

Spring at 50

Roots deep, sucking
groundwater

branches spread
    buds displayed, displayed
    since fall, waiting
    still tight,
    hovering red
    the barely visible filling up, waiting, filling
the water now flowing
flowing up

    all those buds, supported, sustained
    trussed up by the big grown tree

roots spread, seeking, finding rivulets
shimmering up tall strong trunks
    reaching buds,
    buds swelling,
    buds
    new leaves to come
    sheaves of paper, a page a piece

a tall strong tree,
soon to send out shade
spring at 50.

Yield to the earth
yield
    no push, no pushing, no new sprout, not a new blade of grass,
    not a new seed trying to take root, to come up on the forest floor,
    seeing if it will get enough

a mature tree, getting what it needs, year after year, weathers the storms,
has its place
in spring
receives the water flowing up

yielding principle of the feminine, rooted, yielding
    the inner penis full, erect, sturdy, upwards
yielding to the earth
    let it fill me up.

It is no longer the quiet of winter, not that stillness
it is the quiet of hearing the water seep into the cell membranes
listening for the rhythm
it is the quiet of being full
gathering everything for the
thrust forth of birth

I am not concerned with anyone/anything else.
I have to concentrate
attend to the gathering forces
I have to not spill my seed, dissipate.
It is not time for bursting forth,
that is coming.
I do not wish to miss it by not paying attention.
I have to think of myself now, not look too far afield

A mature tree
I do not have to do much
let the water flow
the sun shine
reap the harvest of many years of rooting, plunging the depths,
of reaching, stretching for the sky, seeking

now just bud.

Church

It is Sunday
I go to Church
I park in the parking lot.
The sign says are you
ready
for winter,
pack water, food, careful of ice
early darkness
be prepared to turn back.

I stick to the carriage paths,
the gravel under my feet,
crunching each step
like a heavy soft-shoe.
I do not take the trail to Parkman
or Sergeant, the Amphitheater.
I want to be able to look up
at the bare trees, blue sky,
to look out at the azure sea,
the long horizon and
not watch the ground.

It is cold, winter, three days of below thirty-two.
The grey skies of fall are gone.
The low sun gleams.
The hairs on the bare branches, if you squint
give off the slightest rainbows.
The trees have that brilliant aura of death,
or the pause before rebirth.
What will die, mostly has.
Fall is gone, the letting go almost done.
The brook cascades under a frozen lace waterfall,
ice draped as a curtain across a dark day window.
The water drips behind icicles not quite at rest.
The poignancy only now bearable.

I walk with my shadow, Jungian and real.
My shadow and the gravel crunch
all alone and feeling blue
blue white-ish, clear crystalline air-ish, lung full.

I have returned from where there are only houses, malls and roads,
crisscrossed at right angles, numbered streets and avenues, no names.
The park path has
contours,
just right for nonstrenuous walking, horses, bikes.
Curves following the lay of the land.
It is civilized open space,
the stylized hand of man,
the footsteps a beaten path.

Soon the park will be
the only "uninhabited space"
the wildlife will be squeezed to death.

We will need to take turns
draw lottery tickets
for such a walk.
The tamed park will be all that is "wilderness, natural,"
the only uninterrupted legroom.
We will be asked to leave our cell phones,
beepers at the door.

In Church,
I pray for a
peaceful, joyful
Death
to global capitalism and a return
of humans to our
right-sized place

in the
scheme of things,
however that could flourish.
The gravel syncopates my prayers
I am grateful to walk.

Duality

I.
I will render duality to you
only in these terms

I will see you as mirror, yin, or yang
you choose
only in the living presence of a tree

I will unite the delta reach
of sky branches with earth root
in your capillary bed

I will exhaust myself into
leaf pillows
who dream air into my cells
kissing the sun,
while I and my fellow oxygenators
make compost
from their ancestors

I will flutter thrilled
tendril pink alveoli
with chartreuse baby leaves

I will bark
skin barriers
to contain
water

I stand tall and firm in my place
I ask you to take yours.

II.
I will not talk to you about duality
male female
We are too much alike, bone and sinew

stomach, thyroid, emotions, tool making
It is too myopic a choice,
too humanocentric
I have over-dissected my relationship
to you
born on your fear of needing me
I have studied your ways
with the obsessiveness of a parasite
fighting for a place
in the field
enough
foul play
enough
shitting in the water source
let us stop cutting ourselves down
to the lowest common denominator
a buck today
no forest tomorrow.

III.
I will talk to you of want, desire
of cupping and squeezing breasts
feather brushing the nipple into standing
suck and pull till moaning
of the musty urge to rub my nose in
clitoris, go lip to labia drinking
birth canal ocean, plunging tongue,
fingers, fist,
after
soothing smoothing
inner thigh skin, massaging buttocks
tail bone, back bone, cheekbone,
clavicle, of waiting of wanting of teasing
of riding

I will talk to you of full-engorged penis,
egg sac scrotum pulled, fondled, elongated
play of tongue to tip, tip to epiglottis and again
and again at this speed, that tempo.
after
nape kisses, hair dragged along the spine head to
tail, of wanting you to plunge into me
you parting my thighs with your knee,
that move,
of reaching to you with all of my lips

I will talk to you of the desire
to be locked
in any direction
with whatever accoutrements
of the one I love.

IV.
I will talk to you of
duality
while holding the preciousness
of the millions of years it takes lichens
to make dirt for
a tree
to root in
the steady persistent process of creating life

I will not render opposite your pink rim pushing out of its hood
nor your folded in labia scrotum sacks gesticulating
milkweed seeds
nor do I surrender you off duty once they've landed.

here is the rub.
we two, we do make life
but baby, oh baby
the trees want my exhale
and ooohh do I want theirs.

Naskaeg
(September 11, 2001)

I take Them All there.
anyOne who is someBody
  or going to be Somebody in my life.
  The Ones I love, the ones I want to really know me.
  The Ones I would marry,
  The Ones who are in the category of Best Friends,

I take them All there,
EveryONE.
  Who would jump rocks,
  Who could lie down on granite and know it was not hard.
  AnyOne who could see the shapes of women lapped by the ocean,
    pounded by waves, the granite whale girls, the curves, the nooks,
    the crannies
  AnyOne who could tumble onto small shell beach and know right away
    they could make a rattle, or they want just the yellow or just the
    teeniest tiniest.
  Ones who can see this inlet is made of barnacle shell piles and this
    tide pool is a Microcosm to get lost in. The living barnacles flashing
    out their hair feather tongues, waving in the water catching whatever
    it is they eat and a bigger motion, a finger stirring the pool, a shadow,
    will pull the tongue in and the doors and gates close.

I take all of Them
The Ones who know the performance is watching the round taller-than-us
Rock emerge out of the high tide and submerge again.
I take anyOne who knows a sacred place when they see one.
AnyOne who can feel the weights drop off one by one as we walk across the
  pebbled beach onto the small scattered boulders to the big scattered
  boulders to the pink granite with its fingers and toes.

These rocks, these I recognize.

They are worn away tide by tide, chipped by storms, but to me,
    to my time they stay the same.
I go there over and over again to meet these old friends
    at the edge between the piney green land
    the crashing blue changing sea,
    this pink lace edge of granite.

I lie down.
I give myself to the solid deep vast sound of their breathing and moaning at a
    tone too low for my ears
but vibrates their ancient/future beat into my bones and blood
    grabbing and soothing me across time zones.

"There is more than you, than your worries. We are here, We are here, We are
here inbetween old and on way past you. REST, We will hold Your kind, bring
Them to us. Yes, all of it is true and it is all just a wave that comes and goes
like you, precious one, like you."

Adjudicating Ache

right between the breastbone
traced into the hollows
of spongy bone lattice
the cleavage that veils
matter and etheria
the ravine
my soul's suitcase

this edge-walking
tightrope of ache

falling
    a list of gravities I cannot bear to repeat
arising
    the softness of your rosy cheek
falling
    the spreading begats of violence
arising
    the silver line on the water where the sun burns through the misty grey
falling
    your child's lungs collapsed, my lover's bones losing form
arising
    the golden rays shining

this fence match
grip of ache

arising
    the keening wail
falling
    the down comforter
arising
    the anguished arched neck
falling
    into salt ocean womb bay
arising

      straining to leave the body
falling
      multicolor leaf piles
arising
      beseeching
falling
      yielding

Padding Feet

They walk.
Layers and layers of monks robed in black, in saffron, walking, breathing.
Men.
and women Hidden.
under the robes, fleeing an abuser,
or merely seeking a spiritual life denied because of their vulvas, the
first deep
black hole we all emerge from screaming.
No screaming here
silence, walking, breathing.

They hold the form.
They hold what they call peace.
I trust them walking, breathing simply.

I trust the internal daydreaming/consciousness,
slipping from the breath through the black hole
into images of white curves in dark eggs,
to forms of sky clouds bursting red,
back to the breath,
to the pain in the right knee, to the breath.

They are walking and breathing for us, padding feet.

The bell clangs.
They go to their chopping vegetables for the Brothers (and sisters)
raising grain, hauling water.
Looking now at the
sky clouds flying over the mountains,
the mist rising from the valley,
the water hugging the surface of the brown-grey speckled layered rock as
it is pulled to the ever-crashing surf
they can only hear with the mind's ear.

They hold the form,
The inside is the outside,
all that is between is Breath.

I cannot join them.
I do not want to think only of breath,
my breath of walking.

I have had a breathing practice.
I spent years
in the just not breathing stillness
of a cornered wild animal straining to disappear into the foliage,
in the breathing just enough,
enough for the cells to sustain life like frogs under ice,

I have to scream.
I have to have the blood pumping,
pouring rhythm.
I have to cry singing in my peace.
I have to have raising the dust
cutting the rug.
I have to let my mind fly
to the variegated images
that rise out of my organs sloshing around in my sweet belly
to voice the cries of small soft places.

Riding thru labyrinths of nerve highways
untangling a years worth of L.A. traffic jams,
reordering them into fine unending Celtic knots,
I need a wide berth,

I can now breathe.
Full belly breaths,
panting breaths,
holotropic breaths,
hissing breaths, prana breaths, snot nose breaths.

I can be awed/ conscious
with the breath entering my mitochondria, while
witnessing the pink red purple grey fire sky streaming over the low down
white lights of my town.

I trust with everything the membrane in the middle,
    the breath.
    I sense the padding feet,
    I hear the bell.

Peeling the Onion

Breath
    everything in between
Breath

Breath
    everything,
    muscle, sinew,
    basement membrane, chelated
    receptor sites, cilia,
    granulated leukocyte, terminal
    bronchiole, macrophage, lyosome,
    H2O, NA, Ca, space
    everything named and unnamed,
    everything dreamt, tousled,
    spoken, broken, repaired, every
    predawn thought, séance,
    nuance, every passion, irritation,
    every move
Breath

Breath
    lick, dive, stroke, bellow,
    glisten, snarl, blink of an
    eyelash, tooth gnash
Breath

Breath
    wide horizon line of sea
    sun's arc across sky
    twinkling depth of milky way

    long pause of death
No Breath

Standing with Trees

I haven't breathed easy
since the first time
I heard the chainsaws
cutting the Amazon

Rainforest
full of unnamed species
producer of great
drafts of O2

My lungs, soft pink
membranes
fitting like a glove
over branches and tips

Conjoined twins cut
who gets the heart
who mourns the phantom limb,
who dies?

For St. Patrick's Day

I'm not Irish
but my people were
run over by black crows
hawking blasphemies
against our Brigit.

I'm not Irish
but my people's Boudicca
fecund, ferocious genertix
of us all
was defamed into the
pallid virgin mother, too.

I'm not Irish
but my people's oak grove
was chopped into the cross
for the new hanging hero.

We did not name the wee
people elves or fairies
but every bison, mole
and caterpillar spoke with
Spirit's voice.

We did not tie Celtic knots
or Gaelic speak, but
Psanky, our sacred eggs,
also went the way of Easter.

I'm not Irish,
but Ukrainian, Swedish
English, with a ghost story of
Blackfoot and Jew.

I'm not Irish,
but I am full-blooded

true
Green
pushing up each spring
disrupting every concrete conqueror.

Acknowledgements

Poet and writing teacher Barbara Maria, for inspiration, editing, and guidance and friendship on so many levels.

My writing group Larraine Brown, Therese Hillard, Mary Nevin, Mary Phillips, Jude Spacks, Ellie Daniels, Angel Russek, Coleen O'Connell, and Meredith Bruskin for all the years of listening and telling.

Joan Dury, Kay Grindland, Linda Johnston, Laura Delaney and Marie Fire, for the cauldron of safety and beauty of Norcroft Women's Writing Retreat.

"Currents" editors Wendy Sager, Kate T. Morgan and Susan Davies, and the Body-Mind Centering® Association.

Helena Lipstadt, Kathryn Robyn, Anne Dellenbaugh, Mary Auslander, Joy Vaughan, Jane Burdick, Arifa Boelher, Tom Arnold, Amelia Ender, for faithful years of spiritual friendship.

Jean Hardy, Ham, Jeremy and Violet Niles, and Rachel Donovan for adopted family.

Charles F. Krut, Vicki Pollard, Jan Raymond, Bonnie Bainbridge Cohen, Johnella Butler, Kevin Donovan and Dreams for deep instruction.

David Demere and Debley Foundation for moral and financial support.

My publishing team, Elizabeth Garber, Gretchen Warsen, Elizabeth IlgenFritz and Ray Estabrooke for making the process a smooth paddle.

The wide and interlaced networks of my community, my small town, my colleagues, clients, students, the women's movement, and the peace (inner and outer) movement, all who inspire and sustain me.